WE ARE PHARAOH

ROBERT FERNANDEZ

CANARIUM BOOKS
ANN ARBOR, BERKELEY, IOWA CITY

SPONSORED BY
THE UNIVERSITY OF MICHIGAN
CREATIVE WRITING PROGRAM

WE ARE PHARAOH

Canarium Books
Ann Arbor, Berkeley, Iowa City
www.canariumbooks.org

The editors gratefully acknowledge the
University of Michigan Creative Writing Program
for editorial assistance and generous support.

Cover: Anna Schuleit, *Seated Man II* (detail).
Acrylic, charcoal, and oil stick on linen, 2008.
Used courtesy of the artist.

Design: Gou Dao Niao

First edition

Printed in the United States of America

ISBN-13: 978-0-9822376-5-6

CONTENTS

I

POLYHEDRON 3

THEY KNOW YOU DIE SO WELL 14

SINGULARITIES 17

TROPHIES 18

CHEOPS 19

THUGGEES 21

THE ROOT 26

LYRIKS 27

II

FLOWERHEADS 37

NAUTILUS AND HYENA MEN, LAGOS
(AFTER THE PHOTOGRAPHS OF PIETER HUGO) 39

VICTUALS 42

BONFIRE, JETTY 43

WAVE TROUGH 44

ACREAGE 46

DEPARTURES   48

ACTION PERSISTING PAST RESTRAINT   50

HAYRICK   58

AT THE LECTURE   59

HALO   60

HELL ME DOWN   62

RIDER   64

QUADRANGLE   66

PAGEANT   68

THE PINES   69

III

HORSES OF INSTRUCTION   77

EMERGENCE   79

CLEARING   80

BANKRUPTCIES   83

AUTO-DA-FÉ   84

COAST   86

FOUR SEASONS RESORT, SHARM EL-SHEIKH   87

MOBILE GESTALT   89

WIND MUSKETS   95

LAUDS   97

GROTTO   99

ALBUM   101

SHILL   104

RAG   105

WE ARE PHARAOH   106

ANABOLIC   108

EPITHALAMION   109

PRINCIPLE   111

THREE FALLACIES   113

THE FACULTIES   115

ACKNOWLEDGMENTS   119

I

POLYHEDRON

Intending to begin at the billowing page, the flesh calls back its bulls, the divers arrange themselves, occur as gods (loa) occur, that is, pliant: beds of mushrooms (pendentives) intersected by light.

Think of the bardo as forty-one or 2,700 intersecting *tiles*. The mosaic has a fundamentally Caribbean soul. The under-flesh of a fugue, of cosmic background radiation. A treasure of static is blossoming there. Her wallet is blank, which is incidental. This is the context in which Aida treasures. This is also the context in which childhood attempts to recur.

Avoid nailhead, inset, mouths. Avoid the participle and bread-winning verb. Avoid collusion.

Avoid bulls deranged, fearless in the streets.

Avoid flagstones, reinstatements. Avoid *vendetta*.

An ocean plucks one, two, three, five, seven feathers from its flank—hands them to you. They are intended to highlight sound. With them, you fall back into the life of a painter.

You work construction: Remember that at four in the afternoon February is not accountable to anything, remember the favorable time, the field (namesake). Leviathan in the heart's *salud disminuida*. A peacock stands in the street, shakes out its crest of freshwater. The animus of childhood in the end gets whatever it wants from us; it is not an uncanny burden or dusty crop.

*

Marietta:
your name in strawberry leaves.

One red mouth traveling.

Pentacles like lunettes open through the walls.

*

Speed and *seeing* are the only requisites
to positioning oneself in tradition

or catching rhythm
bare chested, youthful . . .

*

Our binary heritage does not turn dialectically, but differentially through watersheds of fear. Laughter credits us with binary code the color of olives, soil the color of olives. Possession and transformation take place over months or in the time it takes to eat a meal. Tissue threaded across certain occupations: military, police, prison, illness. Compassion trims the moon until it is unseen.

*

The eye is present if the rain is out,
threatens to bend not only reeds

but pitch, guitar, eggs of the macaw.
Not just the river but the shadow of the river travels.

*

I know what it means to burn a bed with lights still startled in
it. Know when five or seven stars are made clear. Sir Stanley
Spencer saw pillows of water. Velázquez saw a lakewater eye
rising into itself.

*

I think the bacchanals of vision are left to sunflowers.

Plaster of aching and fucking

cartels of life

the meat stinks, the vowels are infirm.

The vowels wear dark halos, of which they are ashamed.

I sat beauty in the mud and drank her

the structure of ransom

beside corn fields

unanticipated weather fell

*

this Louis XIV crest I wear
to insinuate my youth
among deadly company

& the soul goes on up the mountain
& the poem's sex cruise

everyone on the beach should
take their bottoms off it's
Dionysian it's
relaxing

*

not smoking glass at dawn but something
men running, bands of light surrounding them
sun   pure body   blistering word

the vultures, blond fins beneath their wings

the sun in tiers . . .

*

"so the bullet that found its way into Roque Dalton's forehead
took its pajama bottoms off
scratched its upper arms felt ashamed
before settling into the worst sleep
in the history of El Salvador"

*

with your lovingly razor-thin feelers,
mr. mosquito
cleaning the trapdoor lashes of the eye

*

the pig emptied, strung up,
smells like wild rain

still

no fun no longer
now the redheads
now I know
what Mann was talking about
& Szymborska
& why Marianne Moore wearing that silly smile beside that pony
is in fact Satanic

*

consider these Botticellis, their hyper-feminine, proto-schizo-
phrenic features, or that the thunder does not have wrists

*

you're close:

hustle hustle

devise devise

*

a mask of pearl
at the oxtail banquet of probability . . .
daylight does not apologize but undresses that fear

*

the cock pecks at human dreams,
causes drops of blood to flow

*

eating souse in London:
I watched the sun
walk in its black wave,
wash dirt from its hooves,
exit the river

*

synthesis of an accurate city—
                    incriminations—
        softened eyes

with increasing interest you watch the stars

*

the shadow of a stone pushed,
flat as an abdomen, beneath the sun

*

steps an egret,
a lash of time in consciousness

*

opening the doors
of the senses,

saw Glory
charge

like a bull

*

if I were a girl

I would be hymnal

if I were a woman

I would be pithy

if I were a husband

I would be a touch-sensitive lamp

if I were a widow

I would uncross turnstiles

if I were a virgin

I would clip energy from fear

if I were a master

I would plant time

if I were a maze

I would wear a prettier dress

if I were a guitar placed in sunlight

I would close my hole

Aida is jealous of the snow

or, the herons and I are blending under searchlights

*

a vèvè travels across the walls
& our Rimbauds burning $7 bills

*

at 7 p.m. in
wildflower summer:

a city inverted and strung
with balloons the color of hospice,

a sea of friends

*

as vocables are stones entire, stone's wholeness, so the wind

pushes back my name

in my hand, stark, with which I carve a whorl

*

say grey carnations threaten skin
& the soul, a fountain through which carnations fall

*

that money is fierce and grows on trees

that the hyena is the only other animal that laughs

that a honeyed crūcifixion has courage

that the wind commissions horsehair sofas

that I dust the cushions out, their flame-retardant thickness

*

I drew myself up
hell smells like shit
surprise
in the pines
a centipede,
a tonsured drunk,
librium, terraces and wrath

*

our enemies
in Sophoclean Emirates
& business cards spraying
from Valentino suits

*

show us what to do when crystals inhabit us

*

follow
the bright meat of the lights
the hard foam life vests flaking red
the clusters of red grapefruit
the façades like blown loa

*

as a pearl Ferrari approximates
the angel of history,
so our mourners shy off
into flatness and ice

*

the day undoes its belts and we have seen
what others have not necessarily wanted to see:

the shells, intricately folded,
of hunger

angel
of history:

a rhesus,
like Brando in an aspirin tree

Hart Crane surfacing,
wrapped in a Haitian flag

*

purple cloud
paper us a will, an instant
of cooling liquid on the tongue

*

tomorrow beauty shifts its name,
swallows landscapes,
rivers—

the seams vanishing across that discourse

*

and the rows of claws retracting in the eye

THEY KNOW YOU DIE SO WELL

I

Love, it's just us, dying to make each other
Inorganic
Love, the safety deposit boxes give silk
The animals that come to drink
At my trough splash around in the bright light
Of my energy
Love, days of pylons, harbors
Love in the boxes, stacks of yellow bills
A heaven of apricots in the blood
Love, mirrors from the mouth and armpits
Stomachs ribbed with light
Blood-orange horizons tapering to cinema
Love stalking the channels
Arriving at auctions in
Masked, immaculate spring
Love at the torso splitting
The pale gold from the yellow

II

I clip the water from the throat
A star on the tongue crawling back into the stomach (give us
Something to eat)
The top of the river is red its sides are brown
Along the river and leaves
Thrust back by wind:
The blond armature, the crushed-gold
Obelisks of the trees, shimmer
Or they are clouds
They are not clouds
They are the tops of bread trees,
Shipments of compact light,
Fragrant light-trimmings
I saw the soul tanning its legs
On the rocks:
Charles August Mengin:
What have you done:
Sapphics:
The masks and dark ladders
Of her breathlessness
Or I think
Shredded banners,
Bertran de Born and the mercs
Spilling out of Limousin like roe:
Black eggs and crème fraîche at sunrise
I think: the pharaoh in her
Camouflage wrappings,
The soul, furled like a wrestler's ear
I think: the beasts eating

Checkered books at noon
Sponsors abound:
Fluent ego deaths, the white dolphins
Of Comme des Garçons,
Álvaro Uribe and the sorcerers
Of tricolored sun . . .
Still my mouth waters beyond hope of reward
Iranian caviar on lingas of ice
And everywhere I go
Unrolling the dry, black carpets of my world
She is at my side in the tent—
A wedding—
Affects like rolls
Of colored gauze—
The violence of their unveilings—
Which is to say that the face
Cut up, crushed, is a vessel . . .
Water falling into open mouths

SINGULARITIES

I

Either way, we make the mistake of looking backward. Repeatedly, the wall—a hand opening its swollen eye on fate. That which arranges itself in backlight acquires a knotted sense of its proportion, an added set of repercussions.

II

Capable, like a boxer's gloves, of mouth-watering speed, we improvise the water of an ethics so cold, so wrapped in sash and clean sensation, it curls in a fantasy of triggers. The face, a portable blackboard (a child's blackboard). The yellow chalk, an arc-en-ciel burning off in your hand. There are traces of the birds that have passed through your open body; of plaster, swept from a bass drum; of an hour of sand-strings and this insistence on travel, on facing there. There, as the tide is drawn in, the pier is held in such a relief you stand as if face to face with the blinding integrity of your death.

III

A spiral of red in the yolk, as from this clipped work: a fruit's clear, poised segments. We interpret the halo's prescience of blossoms shaping the air as they release—cutting, refining the air as they enact themselves.

TROPHIES

I

How can we accommodate these reforms? The nights of bell-flowers are as finished as the hell of water that has unrolled and become news. Pull at the ox's ring and the wall of the sinuses falls down. Pull at the hoop in the eyelid, dormitories are felled. A marriage of fists and kites, the smile is hammered so painstakingly into the gut it forms a ring.

II

I am staring up at a boxing match in which white Everlasts and red Everlasts take on the breakneck speed of cupids. Art Deco façades hem in the open-air courtyard; a black belt of skyline circles off their incandescent white waists. The sunrise pulls level with the sea. The boxers' shadows furl and unfurl, drawing into cups.

III

You open your heart's wings like a bread riot, split the uncooked potatoes on the table with a glance, and eat. You make the hours work like fragile perceptions for the food they get, the warmth they get, for the variable, contradictory spontaneities imposed on their bodies as love or triumph in mistaken assertions.

CHEOPS

Went to the hell of prolapse druggists
to sell my Latin to the technicians of crayons.

Who are angels and liars.
As one who holds the face, a helmet shell,

between the hands—inharmonious,
with the smile like the slit of a wave pulled

toward a formal celebration. You drink
the salt water, the impotable water

of daylight. The voice
folded in an umbrella or a rape.

Through horizon and the bridge,
bricks stamped with the trademark of their provider.

Who are as interested in fulfillment as in
permutations of weaponry, centaurs of technique.

The cock will not be bled
without the ringing of the bets behind it.

The skillet bleached,
reflective in the clear day.

And must have come
with a pump attached to his side.

Who might then—a confederacy—
spread the voice in its wing.

THUGGEES

I

Gets to the party.
Arrives at the party.
Arrives dead at the party.
"On the road, a ghost is dusted glass . . ."
Need bowls of blood to reenact them.
Needs a gleaming red bed to reenact them.
Arrives at the party and collapses on the couch.

"What did you bring to us?"
Sharpens its voice on the concrete,
on the mouth of the breezeway.
"Humor—desertion—trying—looking for you . . ."
"Try 'hard seeing.'"
The hand and throttle fall together.
The hand falls lightly. Aphasia.
The conchs blustery: debt unraveling.

"Covertly, jealously guarding
and attempting to make good; or bent on collection . . ."
"At all costs, believe us."
"Humor."

Hanta in blood-colors through the plowed field.

"As the organs become rags . . ."
Into the mouth of the cave,
across the rug,

flags printed on it.

Eats bronze heart of quail.

Spectacle and rigor.

II

The tempo is
"I cannot see, cannot live."
Casts seed over tile.
" . . . the slice of the body that's foam, a posturepedic,
that turns east, that sets its eye
gazing on the sheeted stone."

"Stop; begin to see; withdraw
horse tail, drenched.
Rough labor.
No rest.
Allergy, no rest;
attrition; until
the debt is recovered."

How useful is a stone?
" . . . extract seed and feed to skinny mutt . . .
  speed—
            armories—
                    El Valle de los Caídos,
necropolis slippery-elegant,
muscled."

How useful a jail?
"Soft, lidding to cities."

Cold blooded, we've come to get a look at you.
You look dry;
teasingly, we scatter
a few drops at the mouth.

Who did not see "drinking
fear from the pelvis of a garuda . . .
Swallow ice chips, modify behavior . . ."
Counterfeited:
" . . . heart in hands, ate of it . . .
squatting, naked, saw
a man."

Will not—(in its given time)
though we desire it—reach us.

Luxury:
revelation cloth
thrown across a crowded room.

How useful is a stone?

"The stomach has become an eye."

III

" . . . would like, (& asks), in asking, an opportunity to
start fresh . . ."

Sand packed into the terraces of the cheeks.

Folly.

By the ribs
            hung &
lowered
into a well.

Persuasion.

In mirror & January
& Jealous Design.

Abandon.

The process of the transformations
has the solemn inexorableness
of a law of nature.

In white sand:

Grace

Stillness

Panoramas

In porous stones,
pumice stones

soaked
in seeing . . .

& would
eat the stones
with white wine and mustard.

THE ROOT

Being active, on the tips of its toes, forking, conversational (best accosted from the side), being hyper-national, elevated, sunk, being foundational, fanning to structure, being hostile, dormant, couched in retreat, being soft vein, mouth, soil and horizon, being disaster and re-architect, plumed through its length, being cluster, spore, sprawl, design and concurrent enaction, being fiber, thirst, hormone, cymbal, lattice and stress, aqueduct and sleeving unity . . .

LYRIKS

I

Find poverty so centered I'm like teak,
phalanx of salt pine advancing its banks.

Stained basketball leathers reflect
horizon's truffles. I find an utterness

of relationship so often entails we are
boyish, find a sunflower on the pharaoh's

lip and seek his council. Exasperated
Barbaras make their way to my

door and in the dawn stand
like book covers drained of light.

Such *sforzando* intent on warping
mind and traffic. As Van Gogh

paints a bouquet of pistols:
I have a caption, two names, two titles:

broadfaced solstice, hallucinating wine.
The mimosas unroll effortless light.

Watch the shadows like sponges
drink together in the rain.

II

Peak hours means a street in Ft. Lauderdale will draw
back its tail and then it's 8:00 a.m.,

radiance as far as Wunderkind
or first year meadowers,

buttresses of cascading hyacinth
into the day's artless and violent

mathematics. No *Timber!*, *Rumpelstiltskin!*,
the feet contemplate levitation.

III

Mollified in winter,
I became a nest,
revelation's field.

Breaded Aloha,
white scales of
hallucination's maille.

The soul in Santa Marta
does nothing but drink.

The heron muscled
from the flame's husk.
Would drag her ball &
chain past Nueva Sept.

In Rome, I felt the snow.
In Vancouver, knees dipped
in flour.

White rum
ices the soul—
& Kyle and Sandro on guitar.

IV

& in Mass Elegance beneath which the soul releases feathery caps
& in lockjaw heaven

& in refined mosquito presentiments
& in ranks of Coptic police

& with the forelock of Janet
& in the DT cage with j. patmos & j. cage

& in the magic of blank tarot
& in *quinine* fleeing *Valhalla*

& in Cuba with grey lice
& China with blond lice

& with Janet all flowers of hell

V

Universal Coincidence
spreads its bars filling all space and light.

The body, sentient candle,
dripping sparks.

Nothing to lose, immolation
of orange and purple wreaths at the limit.

We process sleight of hand, awe, satisfaction,
healing, catalysts, psychosexual pellets . . .

A whirlwind in the street and we can say
I approach you (elide), I event, I wraith, I unfold you.

VI

stones like the sublime
with brandings through it

      stacks of red fruit,
red piss,   gulps of brittle space

weather is not mine,
lust and aggression are not mine

      STELA

      we take the man
      he vomits cowries, we straighten

      the glyphs,
      the four directions note:
      the carvings do not blink

      the ibis, the brick of perfume
            the falcon
      are lethal

stones cut with
berserk lines of mannerist girls

      we walk the shore
light's black booths unfolding around us

VII

& if in windows
if with the gazes spinning light

we are accomplished tomorrow with turnstiles wavering
cameos under each leaf purple and red

I see the souls I know them as they pass
aligned, I am with them
I am beside them

II

FLOWERHEADS

I

Red today, and like a wave-field fanned along the length of
Overtown, a hummingbird-red universe or saturnalia, St. Keith.
Avail us of your administrations. Certain dead president mythotypes
perched on the topmost peak of Watts. Delayed. Abetted
resolutions. I enter the studio and of these sour, convalescent faces:
a logopoeia of flayed reds.

II

What moves along the course of a line must learn the single line,
single statuary's flanked revision of scan, and learn reluctance. Is
hateful. Pools wrath in porcelain. A mandrill clutching the throat in
the billiard hall of Pele. Hasten to work? Wither goest, Ruth in
strange corn: the concise *fft* of levitation. The backs of the knees
sloped like rock elm. The tonal steps of the eyes pushed vaguely on.

III

Boom. Gainsay death metal is a window, ram's-horn ripple. *RZA
shaved the track, niggaz caught razor bumps*. Ascyltus: "To sell 'em piece
by piece, brick by brick, a catch!" Encolpius: "Twice the street value
. . ." Homage gainsays a death-work of preterit lexicons. Tramlines
etched adept, colossal rounded patterns.

IV

Printed "*adagio . . . et in Arcadia ego*." The caryatids of Miami, our
golden bough. Because we endeavor to end in a fuck-all of
resolution: blooms of the crotch and raining credit. THE WORLD
IS YOURS. Laundered ax of draconian abilities. A fast, red-eyed
vireo hollows the duodenum.

V

Of all your Lauds, thinking like a course in statistics but not yet raw
of wheat uninhibitedly pounded not yet sun, wild in your ears.
Then, anxious for news of Mike Tyson. Then I seemed (Thanatos) to
Wifredo Lam (sought) a concise logic revealed, of my situation:
forearms like reddened glass lovely, able to move freely.

NAUTILUS AND HYENA MEN, LAGOS
(AFTER THE PHOTOGRAPHS OF PIETER HUGO)

The reality
is the curve of the wall
and the layer of glaze

as I follow
with my head hooked
into my shoulder.

The reality is
the wall yellows.
The wall yellows

from alpha-hydrangea to omega-white
(all laughter in between
is a breaking of knees).

The wall yellows and the sun,
muzzled, investigates my ribcage.
The earth explores, hyena

muzzled in the streets
of Lagos, the earth
explores my back,

wants to tear my back open,
wants to tear open
my shoulder blades.

In the streets of Lagos
they sell you stiff
black bulbs

like heads of wheat.
The hyenas pace and circle through their
heavy chains. We sell you

stiff little flowers this is
testimony we imagine we are
in this instant stating it.

I must enter the place.
I must stand and act.
I must tread closely to the wall, beak

sloping along my shoulders.
We have sold
our souls for tubs of bleach

we thought would
sanitize the campsites.
Like dry ice,

our souls watered, crushed
into terra-cotta jars and released
in the street.

The motorbikes, the crowds drive
the hyenas crazy. The hyenas
enter our sleep muzzled

with smoke and see us
for what we are. My back
to the wall in the heat

of the day and trying
to shield my neck from the sun
but I cannot. In the street

with the leash,
the chain that's
as large as the thigh

of a child, with the muzzle
that's bright as a vase, dense
as a mullet net bundled up.

With my eyes fixed
and my will tacked inexpertly
to the floor, clasping—the wall

is not rough it is reflective.

VICTUALS

Then *violence* and *practice* and *make it happen*. On the map with the delicatessen that falls through your mind, that shudders in its hide of brick and awning. This is not how we would have wanted it. Village and music box with a little pentacle on its back, and not what we would have wanted for anyone involved. I escape arrhythmias into the heart's normal operation. The valves run smoothly. The hide's parched and pleated but runs smoothly: a bucket of ice and a rhinoceros, a Syrian flag and a recliner. Falling through the rug in the grip of a stomach that sees, we slip past the odds; we feel fortunate. From the bedroom, from closed booths, we plot our victuals. What illuminates the morning better than the souls of the dead?

BONFIRE, JETTY

I get on, nothing to contribute,
and stay happy according to the fire,
nothing to contribute, maze
of loose brick—in inclines
degenerate—bound (higher)—
raking the form from those leaves,
unbuttoning the shirt for those leaves . . .
For the wall, the monument,
Bolivar shattered into rags
& sunlight; unity, "it is our
distinct pleasure . . ."
As the hands topple—affection—
I was, I became, I preferred the sweep
of the water to that fall, I preferred
the jets of pale marble—& the women
they've said to me, & the men
they've said to me, between
the sun's wavering, the water, they say
and remain faceless and beyond my reach.

WAVE TROUGH

Sets the folds in alignment;
this a shallow, a constitution of drops
that moves to displace itself
and unconsciously reverts
to image.

In such a state,
the wave has become a setting—
a table across which cups
with propositions rolled inside them
are passed.

The passage of cups does not limit
the range of potential outcomes,
and yet at no point does the wave
dissolve into abstraction.

The shades
are drawn and we are
overwhelmed by flags
crossing the black divan.

An axis of rotation,
gliding a fraction of an inch
and yet unveiling its total mass.

Advancing, the disc of its body
shimmers. Alighting on the sand,
it reveals itself in a cluster of pulses.

Dilated, it lifts from the sea floor:
fine spokes radiating on a wheel.
It passes between bands of bright
water, a kiss or a plow.

ACREAGE

Stony
in their hemispheres,
the two segments of the brain

lichened on a glass table.
We chart a strategy,
spread the map across

the table and the glass
is darkened. Lens
that aids in seeing

the hawthorn and
ancient ivy. Relief
that aids in plotting

a sail and membrane:
the veins passing across
wheat fields, an etching

in glass of a series of linked
falcons. Over the staggered
vanishing point of the fences,

in rhythmic lines the will
laid flat in a clearing. How
have I come, with whom

have I plotted, what ring
encircles my waist? Your brother
eating glass and your sister

whose feet are swelling shut—
they feed you black radiance
from the run-off of the in-
curled, the sentient light.

DEPARTURES

If I was the breach,
let it be said I was not the pouring forward
of trimly held surface tension,
a blood clot or mirror to be drunk

Let it be said I was not the serpent's
tail of brick sutured up
through the carriage of the spine
and ending in a well-swept mouth:
straw, clay, fire

Let it be said I was not held
beneath living masks
whose translucence darkens to tint
in the tilt toward the light's cascade

Let it be said
we have given no quarter,
but have become
terraces of loose black soil cut
across hillsides in lethal
assemblages of green and yellow tones

Let it be said
I am not this standing in the center of the chest,
as of some squat demigod or golem,
but like one attentive
who brings cups of blood
to lips that will drink

Let it be said
that the Angel's face is flat, like a book
its voice a soft melody, a rustling
as of leaves

Let it be said that when we speak
the inscriptions of the muscle
speak through us in glyphs
of red jade and pearl

Let it be said that a fragrant mask,
as of sandalwood or cedar,
carries the slits of its eyes
over the tops of the trees
into the onrush of the light

Let it be said that the wound
is contoured, rising behind the lips,
that it carries forward in stone and flesh
its muscular and quickened tone

ACTION PERSISTING PAST RESTRAINT

I was tracked down
before I could sleep,
      taken down
in front of a movie theater,
those who found me thought
I had been attacked by animals

             Now, instead of daylight, I see
             cinder blocks, motels, pavilions
             drawing themselves into the earth,
             I see a poisonous midnight and think
             swift, lethal fragments

There is a woman who speaks to me
from the roof of her mouth,

a woman who calls herself
an interlocking of barbells

spread across the stage:
the militia

I think she takes on
certain characteristics from being
assigned to me,
I think *behavior* and together we sharpen
the whites of our eyes

She's the one
who steers me through dust
and pools, the one who guides me
across the city, who helps me
when I can't move my eyes

She turns my head and says,
"There is a post office;
there is a public theater . . ."

The bone chair
           in which she sits
and crosses,
              recrosses her legs

is a value,
a double center,
the twin yolk,
        is prosperity—

does not
divide (is not itself a soul)—
it is a bleeding out

She: "If a wire
sharpens seeing,
         what hones
its beak at the door
but has no tongue?"

In palms the light
in its dark suit speaks
          in motionless bodies—
spills its petals across the floor

                    We refine the human element
                    that locks the stomach
                    in its balance of purpose
                    and play . . .
                              we play—

                    masks of light
                    and intellect,

                    miracled rays
                    traverse the sand

On the mat
with limbs held down,
on the mat
in a play of odds,
    the game-play—
they, who want nothing,
who want our affection,
our sleep

    One valued addition
to the channels,
to the sheets that burn,
to the intestines
fireblasted—
a break in the odds

Who want silence,
reefs linking in façade—
who want alarm, threading us

In addition,
chips of shadow
eating through the skin

In addition,
the white mats
planted, dividing

In addition,
the blood terraced

In addition,
clarity of sunlight

HAYRICK

A sensation of mute nostalgia
that is in fact desire—a desire
to sit with the densely packed
warmth like a shimmering cloud
of blood, like a shield which, moving
toward you, reveals itself as a narrow face.
Not nostalgia, but the vertigo of seeing
a plot of ripe wheat in dead summer:
a membrane of haze through which one
could walk face down, limbs unclenching
along the way. Soft and heavy on the earth,
the rick is neither the anonymity of a pile
of cardboard boxes nor the chiseled intricacy
of a tusk. It is like a bell laid on its side
in front of a chapel. It is oscillations
of thirst (the grinding of teeth)
and contours flared in shade.

AT THE LECTURE

For the landscape *Light and the Viciousness It Absorbs*, certain constellation values: Castor (Surge), Pollux (Mandate), Gemini (Wreathes of Manila Flowers). The speaker has curled into a ball, shielding himself from malignant vibrations in the light. It is a work polished with olive oil. Like a fountain, it uses stone (striation) to cut the value of horizon (soul) in half. It places its caches at successively abridged distances. The sun, wet—weatherless in midday—above locust trees. The billboards, a repetition of the sun's blistering. Once the work has turned against itself, it exhibits newly formed desires. Beneath an armature of stars, it seeks out deltas, anti-luminosities, rings.

HALO

Becomes a decisive body.
Acts on its ends,

which is to say
hands, like cloves,

budding flat.
Cuts a water-wheel

from its body,
a jenny wheel,

Catherine wheels.
It is coastline and,

as such, sheet lightning
issuing in fragile exodus

and armada. Question
what seems less devolved:

flowers wed to hands,
etymologies, stony acts

of will or fate. The center
unravels no more easily

than a stone:
it spreads in leaves,

it erases itself in
strands of brilliance,

it unlocks in florets
through the reflective blackness.

HELL ME DOWN

We take stock of the forearms:
They are like red snapper, slick
And sharp; they are like glass.
You see I am falling through

My pleasure like an intimacy
Of mirrors rubbing against
The face and you cannot uncut
The stomach: it is a die.

Here is the heat because we must begin.
Red rainbow spread like a hawk's gills;
Red rainbow tied off in its black holes
Which dot the ceiling because it is enough.

A nurse raises
Her beak from my chest:
All my vultures are warm
And with gold discs for heads,
All my vultures are form.

Lord find me,
Who is another? Where is the flesh
Of gain? Venture and thighs
Of gold and living glass?

I forget that I consented to wander
To wander by the pier; I consent
That I wander and am like paper:
A black kite wet with night.

Grid I am good and like the Aeon,
A child playing with colored balls.
In the hall because they know me,
The young ones, the eternally. They see

The stela in the flesh of my throat they divine
The throat-rod and its glyphs. Bright to burn
And nurse on cold marrow-like light:
It is midnight and I am speed cut

Into thirds of day; I am threes everlasting &
Hells of foment. Then I stand like eternal resistance
Like hell. No one who walks over this
Ground senses it is sound: look again:

We find ourselves on the shore
And the flame follows us it flows
Through our speaking it is here.
I have failed again, I am no longer I am failed.

I am first to run aground I am seen.
Let us style vital light: New moon again but I am light;
We are not otherwise we are seen.
How shall I stand how shall I be seen?

The morning curled around us like warm like
I am clasped by infinite waters, I am seen.

RIDER

Lemons and red grapefruits,
        priests, blockades, dazzling—a company
of soldiers committed to spending

        more time in the oxygen tent
and less time examining the coast . . . Once
        more we pledge ourselves and break

into the 78,000 seals.
        An index of congratulatory hands
drawing paper cups

        from a clap of groundwater;
today, we were happy . . .
        scalding laughter.

One figure fleeing,
        swallowing a negative;
one with a flash of daylight in his head,

        asking for another.
A beach of primary whites,
        comets, distant lines

of clouds. One comet
        cracked in the skillet;
one $60,000 block of marble

shot at then carved.
The smile traveling along the hand,
　　　a breezeway; along the arm and eye,

a fan; along the face, humanistic sketch
　　　of a lambskin mask
worn clear by vandals.

QUADRANGLE

A slit in the ribs, but nonetheless
so eager to participate

it races itself into the quadrangle
where it's met by packed dirt

and four steel doors, each
at the center of a wall, brilliantly roseate:

doors radiant with flowers. The doors
elaborately cross-beamed. The beams flowing

serrate to a point like taste buds. Each beam
an answer to a preexisting line of inquiry—

notes in a contract. The figure
considers smashing the vases

set beside the doors. Each vase
holds distinct couplings of flowers.

At the north, double violets, lilies.
At the south, angel's trumpets and

gardenias. At the east, iris and rose.
At the west, poppies and dandelions.

The result, an augmentation of what has
already been executed ornamentally in beams:

doors split by budding accompaniments,
by flowers made rhythmically alive.

The figure, tallying its reservations with respect
to an act of senseless violence, determines

that should the equilibrium of door and flowers be disturbed
something would irrepressibly

race into the quadrangle framing
an encounter, or, conversely, the doors

would seal shut, encircling the figure like a host
entering the roof of the mouth before it is dissolved.

PAGEANT

As would be right to assume with breakneck speeds, there is clarity and sedition, a tending to clarity as to a subset of laws governed not by fear but sensate rails, laws of the white tooth, of the golden and the black dove, of capacities bent inward and burning to hybridize. Quite a day to be entombed in these cream-colored blocks. Wholly incapable of time, casuistry, what of these intricately white pigeons chasing around in the painted light, what of the delta that has been unjointed, jointed by a rod in a thoughtful bridge? The mirrors of your veins unfold. What you see in yourself is not presencing but tan beads. A note in the event your capacity does not extend past seeing: *find the wheel.* The clouds are vibrant odds, their light in bridge and penetrative gait neither part of a whole, nor whole, nor a gaze unlocking in indelicate intimacy. A suspicion that we are moving from fair to fair, palace to palace. A suspicion in hot dust, that mandrills and silvery omegas have begun spilling over their colossal argument of names.

THE PINES

I am unable to see. The attendant stretches
in his chair. The chair feels thirst below its feet
in strips of oak. The oak tears away to reveal
rows of red reef. We climb "out on a limb,"
wave a small flag at cars passing by.
An emergency in the woods—
pull over. Woman with a rag for a heart,
child with rags for hands. We have no money
to give you, we're betting you'll be kind enough
to pull off alongside the road. We pray our need
won't turn against us—that in seeing us you
won't shift the balance, start to hunt us down.
We make it to a delicatessen in the nearby
town that splits and bleeds in its hide
of brick and awning. We pass
red brick crawling with threads;
the tailors and seamstresses of metonymy
are out on break, huddled under
awnings. A group of teenagers plays
basketball down the street. Metonymy
cuts off their arms. The hoop closes into itself.
Lush the teenagers all over the bloody street.
Mercy that such strange luck could have
come their way. Mercy that the margins
were too narrow, we had nothing to gain.
We scoured the road for clues to the event
glimpsed behind the trees. The event
was stripped in our listening. The eyes
refurbished it—cell-like, a red chair.

Love, dry mattress with seed packed in it,
began to grow—sent out boughs, leaves.
Love releasing briskly white leaves, lustrous
hysterical white. Love hauled from a motel room,
thrown into ocean water. Love's laughter
and dispersion of evidence. We did not
take our time. We filled our stomachs with souls
and forgot to speak. We were overwhelmed
by the thrust and intensity of action. Waves
hit us in the chest the blood fanned out
from the sternum. Softly spoke then
of a violence farther off—go find help.
Of a heel caught in the mouth of a snake
pressing up from the sand. Above windshields,
billboards, mouths closing around the light
driving above the road in crystalline packets.

There is a heavy wind and I cannot eat.
There is no end to the meal. The charge
leveled against us is that we are bodiless.
I was stuck in the sedan's snow-like leather.
I was stuck with Kai and Dana on the roof
of the Savoy; the red and black bungalows
nearly swallowed us. I was stuck in a tank
feeding packets of diamond dust to thirsty
soldiers. Uncrossing our bones, subject to debt
and loose laws, if we're not realized then at best
rehearsed, skillfully tuned, fanning. If a body,
then fan out the bills. It is impossible that we
should reach the roadside. It is impossible
the levels of virulent water shuttled into us.

We are not rough units of sense we are sand-
blasted. I meet fathers, meet daughters, sons
and mothers in lidless durations on the road.
We imitate the overpasses stretching above
the roads at night. A fan of eyes. Loss of
hope. Bounty. Unable to see. Thus poised,
we evacuate—roughly glitter. Everything

addresses you. The clouds ball up behind
your sternum. You are listening. You see.
A challenge is on its way. It wets its beak.
Because we are flesh, we glide then think.
A mountain of eyes, of rubber bullets,
pours through us, washes clean across
the pines. A wall of seeing passes through
with its shuffling laughter. There are pale-
red pills with pentacles stamped on them,
there are bruises on the road. We are open
to suggestions. The beaches are soft black.
We stall. We unfold soft economies, soft
residences. I am waiting for the answer
to the request the disclosure the spell
that could not listen long enough
to float up its beams of presence and say
this is reality. Laughter. How arcane and
does it not now seem you had a hand in it,
the rose-and-amber carp, a Venus or Adonis?
They restored us; they did us good. Suddenly
the bonds are broken, suddenly the arms don't
work so well. Faint and rapidly drawing closer
to the disease—flag us down. Flay, remove

the roe, lay out the spine. The spine, scales, the
earth are fallow. Platitudes and folly. The earth
is impossibly young. I like to drink black beer,
get fucked up on boardwalks on black sand.
I would sell my name back to myself in
exchange for a ride, in exchange for cords
of order, for a face, clouds—nothing. Who
compels us with their restless batons? Where
is the motive? Where is the mandate? Outlaws
rule these hills. Angels rule these mountains.
We recall, looking up at the violence of spinning sky—
recall a violence that took place in sound alone.
Skilled, we see our arms unlock, souls trained
on fresh estates. We flee from mountains,
from pavilions building across the eyes
in thirst and scarcity.

III

HORSES OF INSTRUCTION

In winter—
        with the front that seems
uncertain
        as to whether
to continue (its
        colored cinder blocks
building toward
        a night)—
with its gusts,
        its gazes
with the fast
        Arubas of the cells
with our thinking,
        our work,
our ointments,
        our noteworthy centers,
our thinking centers—
        we *see*
the energy we eat,
        tear the water up in veins,
drink or stand in the gash,
        listening.
The sun thins and that is its sound,
        that is its speaking:
two puncture wounds in the sun's mask
        meaning
two puncture wounds
        in the stomach
meaning two wounds and a plate

of liver . . .
flash floods are endemic—
         brown snow,
clouds of mosquitoes are not foreign . . .
         I become
tonal blocs, tercets,
         become the tall,
the grey one in
         perfumed black suit,
a host of death's heads, cameras,
         rubies surrounding me.

EMERGENCE

If historical time is a tract of territories, like a field with various plots in rotation, and if each plot is an epoch in human history, say that we are coming out of the terrain of the arcana and entering the terrain of The Grand Tour, say that we have passed from the epochs of corn and wheat and entered The Epoch of the Radish, say that the epoch of wheat passed from the columnar selves of pharaohs into The Epoch of Corn: loa and plumed serpent intercepted by a patois, a cleft palate throwing the sprawl of its wave out, three 6s alighting on a tributary of kernels, ecstasies, labyrinths. In preparation for the new yield, the dromedary of linear time shuttles us forward from crown to heel, positing that which is prior as capsized like a barge under a weight exceeding its capacity to remain afloat. A conceptualization of linear time as a splashing away and of a pushing forward onto a new barge that has miraculously offered itself up—*La Muerte de Dios*. In fact, we have entered The Epoch of the Radish, a crop mummified in the waters of Exile and The Failure of Systems. If we open the as-yet-youthful radish, we see the flesh is unmistakably tinted, for though it may seem an entire epoch has sloughed its hood, that which has passed remains, in Time, both alive and redolently permeable, an intact adjacency whose mediums of soil, wind, water, and sun constitute an omnipresence in power.

CLEARING

I

Ever I believe,
ever I am loved
territory like ink

ever in bloodshot
camouflage spun to inflect
world as rhythm

the soul brays

its task:
leave a jawbone blade
for those St. Anthonys massing
like riot police,
like loss

like chrome
        slaughter,
chrome coffins

as chrome bleeds limb-loosening
radiance, carries us
like Cicero—
        like Helen—

or we desire nothing

II

Angel I've no memory
of unwrapping your thigh to find the book,
but under a plural sunrise
our becoming weapon

I no longer have a face
but terrains, no longer terrains
but the natural grace of fathoms

       planes of movement

       souls surfacing
       in cameos of hard art

small pyramids
mark the perimeter

or to be young
with teething rings for a soul

     with swollen figs
       & souls covered
          in urchins and colored discs

Charybdis:
     a parable of lambs
     unbuttons in the street:
       silence
       fleshed

& held

I inhale
souls, inhale

the height of the rocks,
the pale-black expanse,
the stillness of the clearing

BANKRUPTCIES

To the extent that one can never remember what one was, futurity is a zero-sum game. All practice is a black Miró latching to a wall and a din of clouds chirping at the end of the street. If the time has come—whether we are running or whether we are not running—the light surrounds us with its blond, concentric beasts of prey. Or if I say damage, but you show that you are April; if I say damage and you are April in the midst of institutions, holographs, and the prolonged death of myth. If I say damage and you are April among collectors whose paintings split their skins in rough affection for the light. If you are April and damage waits beneath buildings that shed flames on crowds . . . Each petal of flame feeds a stomach for the time it takes to till a field, to instigate *spontaneous order*. The eyes pitch and whistle, strays in heat. The dogs, in the meantime, with whistles in their hearts entering our yards. And the pigs, the deer, the wildflowers . . .

AUTO-DA-FÉ

It is extraordinary how, stripped of affection,
　　　　　one is able to walk, legs flat, a snake
with its throat in the dust. A tangling of fruits and vases,

　　　　　the shade is verboten. In blinding sunlight,
if over the hills you were to succeed, eyes restive,
　　　　　desire a yellow cloud—if, for your sake,

through your night sweats, if, prevailing, tell us
　　　　　who fell obliquely in the settlement of a fate;
I would take those limbs and,

　　　　　beneath the limes, bless them
with proper burial. The bowl of vinegar,
　　　　　a treatment for this rain-flecked

game of spades. You are dissimilar.
　　　　　That is also a lie. It is your motives that are
as much an exercise in utility and aggression as the hands

　　　　　are diplomats on a mooring ground. We offer
a python's manifold attention.
　　　　　I was a child of The Window. Cored,

we came
　　　　　with cameras,
a heap of lens cloths, filming

a documentary on jails. Shadows defoliating the light,
        we film the crowds issuing, gentle
as starlight, down the halls

        like a ring of keys, a meadow.

COAST

Lethal as ever. We link up. We stay exact. We are the clean cut through the middle quadrant—with box cutters, through pinstripe, though cardboard—we have not yet decided. We are the letters spilling out onto the bare table today. These rash communications. A virus, like carousels of glass; like flame poured on the table, cut cleanly—into quadrants—whether in flagstones or arabesques we cannot decide. Whether a young man walking up from the asphalt or through shadow, we have not yet determined. Look at the waves, they are like blood packets rising, falling. Look at the gulls. Look at the clean shore and the bodies, the parables (I glide a muzzle over the sun's oscillating bands of purple and white).

FOUR SEASONS RESORT, SHARM EL-SHEIKH

Red fan on a train from Sharm el-Sheikh
or Liberia, one history aligning the other:

one in bright, combinatory shelves of towels,
the other, dry banners of sunlight and speed,

the cheeks shaved into a veil. The sun,
rigid in its friezes, says this is a water of fresh events—

momentarily I fail—a smile, compulsions of horns
fluttering in a suit—momentarily, I witness

the drawing of a duration like a fan of water
uncrossed in the heart. Gifted firecoral breezeway,

jackpots of rushing water. Upright, that which by
necessity I will clear away—the figure and its rhythms

desperately put forth. Sewn license of the heart—
other red firmament. There, sun,

walking in an infinity pool with naked feet—
there, futures, zeitgeists of palms that swallow

and lave—there, the sea in its crinkled introspection
of wilds, its maze and bladders. There noons, as we are

children or trumpets—cream-white, satin empathies—
each massing in untenable varieties of hands

that clip our hysterical wills and roses,
retroactive in the sea beside us.

MOBILE GESTALT

A surplus of activity: that we will die offends the dead, who have spent all morning scratching names in our blood. As if the dead were artists.

*

a measure of how I can't wrap my brain around
even these sandals: thinking dies in me,
a toucan's painted face
unrolls across my musculature

*

thinking

the vulture's striated flesh
the current's striated flesh

baroque wings enclose the brain

I am especially receptive to
organic architecture,
deleriants

& am alive one last time today,
having acquired the fluency I want

*

. . . gives a sense of what it means to say the sunlight is full, is black. It is not that the light swallows black bricks, not that the sky appears in aggregate (we are always running). It is that firmament carries us. The lion that is the light and the meat stacked on the table. My head, either way, full of running striations.

*

That I am not this flurry of inlets and appearances tapering, these attractions and folds packed inside the skin . . .

*

then, at her apartment,
something like
a branching red
Picasso on the wall:

plates of hunger
& luminosity

*

but if a heap of rags is bread
& the bread is incandescence,
& if the bread sees

of Utopia's pearly animals:

their feathery meat

their thirst

for infinite occasions

*

I concede
to the wedding-cake
messianisms of August

the rococo body
of the yellowtail snapper
mollifies my eyes

I am at peace

*

or the arrangements we make
to accommodate those numbers . . .

Wifredo, we have no room for your
barbed sternums, your panoramas
whose ghost-pink laps into style

*

these outcrops,
these spiral stairs
that mirror us precisely

as I am able to crack the shell and suck up
the chair's meat, so I become blind,
speak through my movements

*

all the tan knees arrive
at the red chandelier party

our open hands

there is so little to do,
so little to see

seeing wrapped through us like
strips of glass through a safe

I remain a believer . . .

I am best when I am with you

panic, gauze-white scepter buried
in the center of me . . .

but today I am proud,
spilling off in countless directions

today I watch
as the souls come trampling across me

*

with your rainbow tendons, your hard-ons, your orchid face,
your voice little more than a suppuration of time, a lull in which
the eyes heal

the voice stark, near-black, mutely blue, a Portland Vase across
which cameo jackals tangle

or I consider myself châteaux, a Petit Trianon of plaster and
burlap, of paper and hair interlaid, molded into stillness

*

at the horizon

a wall of tankers
a wall of tankers
a wall of tankers
a wall of tankers
a wall of tankers
a wall of tankers
a wall of tankers
a wall of tankers
a wall of tankers
a wall of tankers
a wall of tankers
a wall of tankers

*

I close
the inlets of my face,

but out of the temporal lobes
comes a smoothing brass—

instruments I cannot characterize
like wild honey of the defeated

*

not
        a wall of tankers not
casinos like foliage,
                but a spilling forward from the stomach,
lashes first

*

The moray's jaw
settles on the chest—

flies off

WIND MUSKETS

I

A minimum of amplitude . . . I saw him padding through water, saw what, in another life, might have been an indication of struggle. What we have here, then, is one crashing through planks, trying to stand upright. One who has improbably fallen into an oil slick. I felt my heart drawn shut, stomach boxed and shipped into dunes. I could say that, reaching toward me, he pleaded (he did), but in my memory the event was soundless, a bulletproof cage tipped into an abyssal. What happened was, he never sank. As I was looking at him, something seemed to grab him by the heart and draw back relentlessly, as on a rope.

II

The one who is me at that particular point in time is walking the streets of Miami Beach toward the one who is here now, folded up like a blanket, with you. A pulse drives him on—a libidinous streamer is tied to his wrist. How to speed along and so denote a sense of urgency, or paint the face and let it glide up not just in front of you but from within you, a face unfolding out of your body to address you, face to face? Entering the Raleigh Hotel, he is struck by blasts of air-conditioned air that fan out across the pale steps. We determine that going no farther— and yet, too, continuing onward—results in numbing wounds. Entering the lobby, the stacked light gives way to gelded suede and dark. Rest assured, I am crossed, I am crossing the lobby and entering the hallway, announcing my intention as this: the fourth floor. He is white noise ringing its hands. A nosebleed. I am the noise that is pleading to the noise that is listening—my insolent varieties of actions bonded together, guided into this hotel room, this present noise. The urgency, the what-we-must-do, is to remain cool while waiting. I watch the Greyhound blimp cutting against rose sky: *Dania jai-alai, every weeknight.* The jai-alai sling of involuntary memory lays its crack into the wall. Once again left to my own devices when I would so much rather subsist on the generosity of others. This, the waiting, is a chord of inexplicable anguish breaking into planks.

III

I anticipate that something should come, unlocking the room and driving us out of the hotel to satisfy what has been promised to us by these transactions. The one who is the key to these transactions enters the room. The one who is the key to these transactions enters guiding a herd of familiar actions. There is nothing here other than the ear-piercing definition of one among friends who, like a billfold passed from face to self and other, has capitulated under the weight of a nod. May as well find myself a corner of the room in which to sleep, or are the apartments still vacant? I could throw down a sheet and wouldn't be more than a day . . . The one who enters the room, however, is like a watercolor painted on a jade bowl and I am here to listen here to say if nothing else *have we not come together to strike a deal?*

LAUDS

Stranger, our estate may
revalue you. You become

current and the jetty stones'
gray revelations in multiple sails.

Beside us, you are better off
transient—in debt.

To look a chrysanthemum
dead in the face
and divine its nature:
the ice of such drywall
like a lattice of metaphysics.

You eat from raised shells,
cutthroat shells
that backtrack,
      & each
with something to say.

The horizon,
from its closed tripod,
slides loose of its encasements,
pressing farther and deeper
among spires, cleanly.

Elegance and willingness,
their bi-part elocution,

lock at the wrists
and divide.

Moored, you are
too intimate in us.

A boardwalk,
the streets,
the red carpet
of sunrise planted
in an acre of your back.

GROTTO

A sail
composed of equal parts
sand and legibility.
If the light is
strong enough,
the task being
to erect such canvas
in partitions. An infinite
distribution of planks.
Infinitely, each plank
fixing into a slot
and where
judiciousness
      aligns need:
the satisfaction of hunger;
where light becomes bare wall, grooves
spontaneously aligning rills:
the satisfaction of thirst.

Attending
to structure in failure,
I open my arms and receive
a ransom of planks.
Attending to structure
in satisfaction:
vacancies spreading
like the wing bars
of an ivory-breasted finch.

As in a derelict hotel,
the eye is seized
by a pulse of water,
by a roll of carpet
like thirst, by light
like an eel seamless
through bone-
white reef.

The clear light of the overpasses
and the pale light of billboards
veils us.

ALBUM

Dread has his hands on you.
The way he lives looks good
and you believe him. The way
he moves looks good and you
believe him. Gray gel leaking
from a hive, dread looks good
but should not be confused
with the balls of the feet.
The aorta rushes to interject.
The aorta, the gray cloud—this
disingenuous ambiance. In an

abandoned warehouse in Berlin,
hives, hearts, hands, red rags,
they flee distorted. The party
goes on till noon. In the
heat of the day running until
the liver, kidneys, lymph do
their job and clear the brain,
drain the brain. It is
the eyes that unfold

cameos of blood &
desperation. Behind the wall,
between golden kernels,
we see better, we search
our names out beneath each brick.
We are unable to see, but stand
streaming in our black suits.

Our cousins find us at the heart of
the building in dampened patches.
The moss is white. The sun, white.

The streets resemble us. Feel
the muscles in my calves, the tread
of the soles, the instinct toward
preservation. I will prevent
myself from swimming, seeing;
let the sun cut the yellow pearl
from the base of my eye. What
is weather? Our superstition,
the reassertion of our existence

in markets where family
seeks us out. What is breath?
Soul's lens, soul's convex face
gritting and masking. Is this good weather
for a performance? Do we not see?
What is the blood? Trim stair,
covenant and seal,
flowing lectern. The weather does not
delay, it designs. What is

the skin? The inability to lie,
lurid breastplate, not
world and not souls but mind,
art, slick padding. Would
you agree one intends us,
stops with us, one
prohibits and prevents us from

sight? Though I desired to be seen,
wanting it, it was, as by conveyor,
moved farther and farther off by my
syntax. I learned

the mandate: to commit. When
the torso is rolled, when the smooth
angel's trumpets are mixed in
with the black parts of the body,
the body sees. What is the torso's
seeing? If not weather, then
cloth, skin, the ripple
of monuments—sphinx first
skillfully then recklessly reshaping
its foam-white parts.

If you're willing to lose a single hue,
why not the grain, why not
the full, floral deserts? I am
unable to intend them. The eyes, gray,
the eyes a refreshing of gray
bullion as the lashes spill dis-
information into the luminosity.

SHILL

I hope the desert is just a rest stop, and that, my dears, above
all else, we appear sophisticated. Have you ever seen genuine
porcelain fixtures? Lately, all the eggs hold a dot of blood and
lately in films a sophisticated sorcery flows over the ceilings and I
see it. Such a sorcery has made the rooms flaxen and dry, like
candy. Such a sorcery has made the infinity of holes fanning out
beyond the ceilings swoon and purse a little. Still there is a word
for what I am seeing, a word for what I've not seen: stacked
cakes like cocaine or coal pedaled along on a wood cart. This to
warm the rooms by. The word? *Errant*, perhaps. The word leading
us from one plank to the next over the undisturbed surface of the
channels. As the planks lay out, our steps pour out. As the green
koi and the blond koi have plans for us, so I step off the improvised
barges and face the pines in their compact freshness, so I am like
a wound folded back from either side of the flesh that has opened
me. I bear forward—and may I continue to bear—mermaid-like,
specter-white, forward as on a prow—toward figures of rope
and cuttlefish—toward the continuing parabolas of green dialects.

RAG

If awnings collapse into the earth
and reveal jars untouched for an age

If I brush the soul from your face and distract you
with the scent of mineral oil and cashmere

If the streets crowd with boys spilling
from window shades—raw brown
pavers stacked up

Then the birds of paradise also hang
from bits of wire around their feet,
by scandalous holes in their necks

WE ARE PHARAOH

I should have said the iris
In its network of evictions

I should have spoken
More softly

We no longer fear,
We are no longer—

Our throats
Are inadequately sexual

I've exchanged my reflexes
For a $6,000 suit

The color of oxygen
And silence

We split silence's red liver
And became conscious of our art

In the streets, a universal:
It is accurate to say

We who eat at the table,
Speak at the table, see

At the table,
Are painful

Dilations and constrictions
Made bright by

A dominant
Impulse: to survive.

ANABOLIC

I

draws the style of yellow crowns
from the slit of the mouth

the style of yellow crowns
from an upwelling of lashes

the flared lip of the conch
from ponderous bazaars

II

in its uprushing and poised sails, the moray
a little loaf of bread falling into slices
of its own volition . . .

lest in
crushed black incense,

jasper and rigorous sun

lest, aligning in soft proportions,
extrude veils and fires

EPITHALAMION

At once this dragnet of cousins
Whips its way into your presence saying
None of them among us. They are
Oracles on the court of midnight,
The tight filigree of a mind or your
Splashing around in, your pandemonium
Of copper graffiti inexpertly put up.
They make weapons of furled hands.
"We will walk, but our bones will carry
Ribbons of lead, or we will, like
Acrobats mill-headed in 3s (3 blades,
3 hips, 3 tongues), answer to what comes
Before, what comes before?" Eleousa,
Master of Dark Eyelids, eye opening
Like a fennel seed, you are generous
Or are you not, do you shore up and
Wink at the soul? What does the soul say
Other than "my divorce from . . .," "tan
Holiday . . .," "smoking crystal in teak rooms . . ."
But should have asked, "What do you
See?" The sun a sequence of fans, a bridge,
Only so exquisitely cabled as to make us
Still—shall we fall
Or travel between bridges
Among the robust, sane clouds,
A face cut from smoke, heat, and light?
The sun, dancing in a vial, the initial
Memory of what it was to be born—
Doberman of a sheer-white universe—

To school out—the audacity of rising
Without name or color to new rooms,
New youth, fruitful, born singularly
To precise moments not in epiphany
But duration—as under new weather
We become—in action, receive—our
Bodies uncasked like umbrellas under
The flamingo-red light of the racing day.

PRINCIPLE

Arrive at the best principle,
little gravesite, pyramid
of limbs. Scan furtively
up and down: perhaps
you catch a tile in the unbearable act
of watching you. Unbearable
because it is loving and because
loving is unmanageable, a flag
swarming with colors.
The smell of the spirit,
like wet clothes left
in the sun at a public pool,
is also the color of the confused,
the busy flag. Every fifteen minutes
until 11 a.m., then every hour until 3 p.m.,
departures: "Love I love to sit here with you
and to eat strange meat . . ." Thus and so,
and other things,
said while gazing from the benches
of the ferry, that make us laugh.
What you saw on arriving was a crescent
of black sand flanked
with reeds. What you saw
was the vacuity hinted at
in passengers on moving walkways
flowing through air terminals in
man-of-war light, a primary violet
couched in weeds. Still the pavilions
close up their slats

and in this they resemble
souls, buckets of
ice. Who is so human as to
know the thousand limbs, who is less
than human in this forum, is it you
I'm speaking to, you with the bare feet
in the last form, in full form—I was
in a conference, my lieutenants
like pincushions swept into the walls . . .
I was bleeding, I wanted
to stand and show you that in my chest
were compartments, riots of boys
scratching at their necks, I wanted to
show you that here were all sorts of things
that might have been of use to you.

THREE FALLACIES

I

Bled, the fields divest, the streets divest, the clouds divest. I help you take that rag into your mouth, that strip of plaid into your thought. Or it is that Caesar slides his hand along the horse's pale neck in the twilights of incompossibility. Caesar in a series of bridges, in the huts and arches of his incompossibility. I am at work in the rain, in the golden light of the rain's gaze and the street's tremor: the pink candles that surround the body.

II

Between pillars of rose, between smooth pillars of thought. If seeing is assertion, I intend to walk. Or I am in the breezeway and the animals are brittle with folds, brains proleptic between intentionality and placement. Utopias of equally bashful line lengths understand: a cell is not a cell, the soul is lined and infinite light. The dolphins lap beside the docks like flattery, horns like tangled ideations. Who says the horns are as soft, the tooled-white egrets are as soft? The vultures first inhale, then release, the slits of their backs in the early light.

III

In irruption of pearls I considered myself fortunate. Bricks of perspectival shining built us a kiln and the means to make more bricks. If we begin to track the clouds, we become a tree of folds and the mind's releasing rimless ecstasies through it. If we follow the vultures circling at that height, we inhale soft black down from beneath feathered slits. If we drift through pink Soutine streets, we prefer city centers—the multicolored candles along gutters and under storefronts.

THE FACULTIES

Madonna of base erudition,
splintered in bars—perfunctory,
you came with the idea your
organs would (did) follow.

They who appear dutiful,
students who have sequestered us—
arraigned, like sunlight in timothy.
One in a cage, one of us
on a barge sailing by,
one swallowed like a tusk,
one bird of paradise,
one in garrets, stockades
gathered along causeways
in the ribbon-shuttered center
of the vast city—

    We who wait
for a cyclone to draw
its eye of granulated dusk
into completion, for a flag
to branch with multiple rays
of thirst from the center of a well.

We have opened our lives
upon silence and the bridge.

ACKNOWLEDGMENTS

Grateful acknowledgment is made to the editors of the following journals in which some of these poems first appeared: *1913*, *Action Yes*, *American Letters & Commentary*, *BafterC*, *Green Integer Review*, *intersection(s)*, *The Modern Review*, *Octopus*, *Quarterly West*, *Volt*, *Web Conjunctions*, and *Zoland Poetry*.

"Quadrangle" received a Gertrude Stein Award for Innovative Poetry (2006-2007).

"We are pharaoh" is taken from *Financial Times Deutschland*, quoted in *Solution 9 The Great Pyramid* (Ingo Niermann and Jens Thiel, eds.).

In certain places poems in this book quote from, adapt, or are otherwise indebted to William Blake, Paul Claudel, Stephen Crane, Gilles Deleuze, Bryna Freyer, GZA, Heraclitus, John Keats, Gottfried Leibniz, Friedrich Nietzsche, Petronius, Psalms, Arthur Rimbaud, V. Rossi, and Daniel Paul Schreber.

Robert Fernandez was born in 1980 in Hartford, Connecticut and raised in South Florida. He is the recipient of fellowships from the Iowa Writers' Workshop and the University of Iowa Department of English. *We Are Pharaoh* is his first book.